I GOT THIS

The Self-Empowerment Journal

Danielle Lee, LPC-S, M.Ed

Copyright © 2022 Danielle Lee
All rights reserved.
ISBN: 978-0-578-95384-7

Copyright

One definition quotation is taken from Merriam-Webster's Dictionary Online Copyright 2021. Used by permission. All rights reserved.

Quoted sources: Elbert Hubbard, Buddha, Viktor E. Frankl, Maya Angelou, Jack Canfield, Dale Carnegie, Nelson Mandela, Robin Sharma, Sarah Addison Allen, Eric Thomas, Germany Kent, Ralph Marston, Mike Hawkins, Mother Teresa, Michelle Obama, Stacey Abrams, Ernest Lee Thomas, Confucius, Charles Buxton, Eleanor Roosevelt, Oscar Wilde, Helen Keller, Mark Strand, Sanhita Baruah, Carl Young, Beyonce', Oprah, Kerry Washington

Designs, editing, and production by: Cassidy A. Lee Press, LLC.

Images used under license from Canva.com

No part of this publication may be reproduced, stored in a retrieval system, or transmitted in any form or by any means, electronic, mechanical, photocopying, recording, scanning, or otherwise without the prior written permission of the Author. Requests to the Author for permissions should be submitted to Danielle Lee at the following email address: SolutionFocusedConsultingBR@gmail.com.

Introduction

Merriam-Webster's definition of self-discovery is, "the act or process of gaining knowledge or understanding of your abilities, character, and feelings" (Merriam-Webster.com. Merriam-Webster, 2021).

It may seem like a scary topic, right? In reality, you are the only person who really knows who you are. You are the expert in your life. Self-discovery gives you the opportunity to look at an uncovered path you never noticed. Whether it be dreams, values, or talents, you get to become more aware of your inner self. Learning more about yourself causes an increase in insight and intuition. You will be able to tell if a situation is truly meant for you.

These journal prompts are here to start your path to self-discovery. These prompts give you the opportunity to reflect on situations and relationships in your life and how they shaped you today. You can learn from your past experiences and use them as an opportunity for growth.

Introduction (Cont.)

Also, these prompts are here to help guide you back to yourself. Oftentimes, we get caught up in our daily work/life tasks, and we forget what we used to enjoy. Now is a great time to remember happier moments. Allow yourself to sit in those feelings and be encouraged that they can come back around again.

Lastly, as a big advocate of self-care and empowerment, I want you to remember that you should not pour from an empty cup. You must pour into yourself as much as you pour into others. You are here in this world for a reason. Live to your fullest potential every day.

> "THE SECRET OF GETTING AHEAD IS GETTING STARTED."

ELBERT HUBBARD

Self-Discovery Prompt 1

Write a journal entry based on this prompt:
What are things you want to pour back into yourself?

_____
_____
_____
_____
_____
_____
_____
_____
_____
_____
_____
_____
_____
_____
_____
_____
_____
_____
_____
_____
_____

> "DO NOT LOOK FOR A SANCTUARY IN ANYONE EXCEPT YOURSELF."

BUDDHA

Self-Discovery Prompt 2

Write a journal entry based on this prompt:
What would your higher self look like?

> "WHAT YOU ARE IS WHAT YOU HAVE BEEN. WHAT YOU'LL BE IS WHAT YOU DO NOW."
>
> BUDDHA

Self-Discovery Prompt 3

Write a journal entry based on this prompt:
What are five things you love about yourself? Describe why.

_____
_____
_____
_____
_____
_____
_____
_____
_____
_____
_____
_____
_____
_____
_____
_____
_____
_____
_____
_____
_____
_____
_____

"LET US RISE UP AND BE THANKFUL, FOR IF WE DIDN'T LEARN A LOT TODAY, AT LEAST WE LEARNED A LITTLE, AND IF WE DIDN'T LEARN A LITTLE, AT LEAST WE DIDN'T GET SICK, AND IF WE GOT SICK, AT LEAST WE DIDN'T DIE; SO, LET US ALL BE THANKFUL."

BUDDHA

Self-Discovery Prompt 4

Write a journal entry based on this prompt:
Describe why you are a gift to the world.

_____
_____
_____
_____
_____
_____
_____
_____
_____
_____
_____
_____
_____
_____
_____
_____
_____
_____
_____
_____
_____
_____

"OUR LIFE IS SHAPED BY OUR MIND; WE BECOME WHAT WE THINK. JOY FOLLOWS A PURE THOUGHT LIKE A SHADOW THAT NEVER LEAVES."

BUDDHA

Self-Discovery Prompt 5

Write a journal entry based on this prompt:
What is your favorite song? How does it make you feel when you listen to it?

"WHEN WE ARE NO LONGER ABLE TO CHANGE A SITUATION, WE ARE CHALLENGED TO CHANGE OURSELVES."

VIKTOR E. FRANKL

Self-Discovery Prompt 6

Write a journal entry based on this prompt:
What is your dream vacation? Describe the place, people, and activities you would do.

> # I AM WORTHY; I AM IN CONTROL OF MY LIFE. I AM SAFE, I AM GRATEFUL, AND I AM MEANT FOR SO MUCH MORE.

SELF-AFFIRMATION

Self-Discovery Prompt 7

Write a journal entry based on this prompt:

Write down a positive letter to yourself to reflect. Read it during your bad days.

"SUCCESS IS LIKING YOURSELF, LIKING WHAT YOU DO, AND LIKING HOW YOU DO IT."

MAYA ANGELOU

Self-Discovery Prompt 8

Write a journal entry based on this prompt:
What would your self-care look like?

_____
_____
_____
_____
_____
_____
_____
_____
_____
_____
_____
_____
_____
_____
_____
_____
_____
_____
_____

"COURAGE IS THE MOST IMPORTANT OF ALL VIRTUES BECAUSE, WITHOUT COURAGE, YOU CANNOT PRACTICE ANY OF THE OTHER VIRTUES CONSISTENTLY."

MAYA ANGELOU

Self-Discovery Prompt 9

Write a journal entry based on this prompt:
What are five things people don't know about you?

> "IF YOU ARE ALWAYS TRYING TO BE NORMAL, YOU WILL NEVER KNOW HOW AMAZING YOU CAN BE."
>
> — MAYA ANGELOU

Self-Discovery Prompt 10

Write a journal entry based on this prompt:
Write a mayday plan for when nothing seems to be going your way. (For instance, what things can you do to get out of your funk?)

"EVERYTHING YOU WANT IS ON THE OTHER SIDE OF FEAR."

JACK CANFIELD

Self-Discovery Prompt 11

Write a journal entry based on this prompt:
Who are the most important people in your life? What makes them so important to you?

"INACTION BREEDS DOUBT AND FEAR. ACTION BREEDS CONFIDENCE AND COURAGE. IF YOU WANT TO CONQUER FEAR, DO NOT SIT HOME AND THINK ABOUT IT. GO OUT AND GET BUSY."

DALE CARNEGIE

Self-Discovery Prompt 12

Write a journal entry based on this prompt:
What is one trait you wish you had? How can you work at developing this trait for yourself?

"I LEARNED THAT COURAGE WAS NOT THE ABSENCE OF FEAR, BUT THE TRIUMPH OVER IT. THE BRAVE MAN IS NOT HE WHO DOES NOT FEEL AFRAID, BUT HE WHO CONQUERS THAT FEAR."

NELSON MANDELA

Self-Discovery Prompt 13

Write a journal entry based on this prompt:
Write a poem describing your day.

❝

"THE FEARS WE DON'T FACE BECOME OUR LIMITS."

ROBIN SHARMA

Self-Discovery Prompt 14

Write a journal entry based on this prompt:
Write 10 things you are grateful for.

"SHE UNDERSTOOD THAT THE HARDEST TIMES IN LIFE TO GO THROUGH WERE TRANSITIONING FROM ONE VERSION OF YOURSELF TO ANOTHER."

SARAH ADDISON ALLEN

Self-Discovery Prompt 15

Write a journal entry based on this prompt:
What is your favorite animal? What traits do you like about it? Does it remind you of yourself?

"YOU CANNOT AFFORD TO LIVE IN POTENTIAL FOR THE REST OF YOUR LIFE; AT SOME POINT, YOU HAVE TO UNLEASH THE POTENTIAL AND MAKE YOUR MOVE."

ERIC THOMAS

Self-Discovery Prompt 16

Write a journal entry based on this prompt:
Listen to a guided meditation soundtrack for 10 minutes. Make sure you are in a quiet environment. Write down what you saw and your thoughts.

"IF YOU CAN'T STOP THINKING ABOUT IT, DON'T STOP WORKING TOWARDS IT. STAY IN PEACE, YOUR BREAKTHROUGH IS COMING."

GERMANY KENT

Self-Discovery Prompt 17

Write a journal entry based on this prompt:
What are three things that make you upset? Why?

"THE DIRECTION OF YOUR FOCUS IS THE DIRECTION YOUR LIFE WILL MOVE. LET YOURSELF MOVE TOWARD WHAT IS GOOD, VALUABLE, STRONG, AND TRUE."

RALPH MARSTON

Self-Discovery Prompt 18

Write a journal entry based on this prompt:
Reflect on a bad day. What made the day so bad?

"YOU DON'T GET RESULTS BY FOCUSING ON RESULTS. YOU GET RESULTS BY FOCUSING ON THE ACTIONS THAT PRODUCE RESULTS."

MIKE HAWKINS

Self-Discovery Prompt 19

Write a journal entry based on this prompt:
Write down 10 positive self-affirmations.

"I ALONE CANNOT CHANGE THE WORLD, BUT I CAN CAST A STONE ACROSS THE WATER TO CREATE MANY RIPPLES."

MOTHER TERESA

Self-Discovery Prompt 20

Write a journal entry based on this prompt:
Write down five things that are non-negotiables you need for a successful relationship.

"SUCCESS ISN'T ABOUT HOW MUCH MONEY YOU MAKE. IT'S ABOUT THE DIFFERENCE YOU MAKE IN PEOPLE'S LIVES."

MICHELLE OBAMA

Self-Discovery Prompt 21

Write a journal entry based on this prompt:
Describe the last time you felt lonely? How did you overcome those feelings?

> "BE AGGRESSIVE ABOUT YOUR AMBITION. DO NOT ALLOW SETBACKS TO SET YOU BACK."
>
> — STACEY ABRAMS

Self-Discovery Prompt 22

Write a journal entry based on this prompt:

Write down five regrets. After you write them down, tear the page out and destroy it. (You can tear it up or burn it but be careful). Make sure you let go of whatever you wrote down).

"NEVER, EVER SPEAK ANYTHING BUT GREATNESS IN YOUR LIFE NO MATTER WHAT YOUR CIRCUMSTANCES ARE. THE ONLY REALITY IS THE ONENESS WITH YOU AND YOUR CREATOR."

ERNEST LEE THOMAS

Self-Discovery Prompt 23

Write a journal entry based on this prompt:
Describe the one person you trust and why.

> "THE MAN WHO MOVES A MOUNTAIN BEGINS BY CARRYING AWAY SMALL STONES."

CONFUCIUS

Self-Discovery Prompt 24

Write a journal entry based on this prompt:
Describe your perfect day.

"DON'T LET THE HARD DAYS WIN."

UNKNOWN

Self-Discovery Prompt 25

Write a journal entry based on this prompt:
What is your favorite food? How does it taste? Smell? Look?

"YOU WILL NEVER FIND TIME FOR ANYTHING.
IF YOU WANT TIME, YOU MUST MAKE IT."

CHARLES BUXTON

Self-Discovery Prompt 26

Write a journal entry based on this prompt:
Write down 10 things that made you smile today.

"DO ONE THING
EVERY DAY THAT
SCARES YOU."

ELEANOR ROOSEVELT

Self-Discovery Prompt 27

Write a journal entry based on this prompt:
What would your life look like five years from now?

❝

"TO LOVE ONESELF IS THE BEGINNING OF A LIFELONG ROMANCE."

OSCAR WILDE

Self-Discovery Prompt 28

Write a journal entry based on this prompt:
What motivates you to keep going?

"WALKING WITH A FRIEND IN THE DARK IS BETTER THAN WALKING ALONE IN THE LIGHT."

HELEN KELLER

Self-Discovery Prompt 29

Write a journal entry based on this prompt:
What do you need to do to love yourself more?

❝

"I AM BRIMMING WITH ENERGY AND OVERFLOWING WITH JOY."

SELF-AFFIRMATION

Self-Discovery Prompt 30

Write a journal entry based on this prompt:
What things do you do (mentally or physically) to take care of yourself?

"WHEREVER YOU GO, GO WITH ALL YOUR HEART."

CONFUCIUS

Self-Discovery Prompt 31

*Write a journal entry based on this prompt:
Describe your favorite childhood memory.*

_____
_____
_____
_____
_____
_____
_____
_____
_____
_____
_____
_____
_____
_____
_____
_____
_____
_____
_____
_____

"THERE IS A SPACE. IN THAT SPACE IS OUR POWER TO CHOOSE OUR RESPONSE. IN OUR RESPONSE LIES OUR GROWTH AND OUR FREEDOM."

VIKTOR E. FRANKL

Self-Discovery Prompt 32

Write a journal entry based on this prompt:
Describe one movie from your childhood you used to enjoy watching. What feelings do you have after thinking about it?

"THE FUTURE IS ALWAYS BEGINNING NOW."

MARK STRAND

Self-Discovery Prompt 33

Write a journal entry based on this prompt:
What is one thing you are good at and no one can take it from you?

> "LIFE IS, AT TIMES, TOUGH. AND ALL WE NEED TO DO IS TO PROVE THAT WE ARE TOUGHER THAN IT."

SANHITA BARUAH

Self-Discovery Prompt 34

Write a journal entry based on this prompt:
Describe the people who raised you. What values did they teach you?

> "UNTIL YOU MAKE THE UNCONSCIOUS CONSCIOUS, IT WILL DIRECT YOUR LIFE, AND YOU WILL CALL IT FATE."

— CARL YOUNG

Self-Discovery Prompt 35

Write a journal entry based on this prompt:
Write one lesson from your childhood that shaped you into the person you are today.

> "I BASE MY WORTH ON WHAT'S INSIDE MY HEART, NOT ON WHAT'S ON THE OUTSIDE OF IT."

SELF-AFFIRMATION

Self-Discovery Prompt 36

Write a journal entry based on this prompt:
What things can you do to make yourself feel safe?

> "BE HEALTHY AND TAKE CARE OF YOURSELF BUT BE HAPPY WITH THE BEAUTIFUL THINGS THAT MAKE YOU, YOU."

— BEYONCE'

Self-Discovery Prompt 37

Write a journal entry based on this prompt:
Describe what things make you feel more connected to people.

"

"SELF-CARE ISN'T SELFISH."

SELF-AFFIRMATION

Self-Discovery Prompt 38

Write a journal entry based on this prompt:
How can you be more kind to yourself?

"BREATHE. LET GO. AND REMIND YOURSELF THAT THIS VERY MOMENT IS THE ONLY ONE YOU KNOW YOU HAVE FOR SURE."

OPRAH

Self-Discovery Prompt 39

Write a journal entry based on this prompt:
Finish the following statement: If I knew what I know now, I would...

"I THINK IT'S REALLY IMPORTANT TO TAKE THE STIGMA AWAY FROM MENTAL HEALTH... MY BRAIN AND MY HEART ARE REALLY IMPORTANT TO ME. I DON'T KNOW WHY I WOULDN'T SEEK HELP TO HAVE THOSE THINGS BE AS HEALTHY AS MY TEETH."

KERRY WASHINGTON

Self-Discovery Prompt 40

Write a journal entry based on this prompt:
In three to five paragraphs, write your life story.

Worksheet #1
Thought Record

A thought record is a method of documenting and analyzing your emotional state. It can help you understand your emotions and the relationship between your thoughts and feelings.

Instructions: Use this chart to log your emotions and thoughts, as well as answer questions about what might have influenced you to feel the way you do.

Thought Record

Situation	Thoughts	Emotions	Behaviors	Alternate Thought

Worksheet #2

Daily Mood Tracker

A daily mood tracker is a goal-directed, mood monitoring method. It can be useful for anyone who wants to learn more about their moods and improve how they feel. It is also a valuable technique for people who have trouble expressing themselves. In short, the daily mood tracker provides valuable self-reflection opportunities.

Instructions: *Use this daily mood tracker to help document the ups and downs of your moods during the day.*

Daily Mood Tracker

	06:00 - 08:00	08:00 - 10:00	10:00 - 12:00	12:00 - 14:00	14:00 - 16:00	16:00 - 18:00	18:00 - 20:00	20:00 - 22:00	22:00 - 00:00
Happy									
Sad									
Angry									
Excited									
Anxious									
Tired									
Other									
Notes									

Worksheet #3

Self-Care Checkup

The self-care checkup is a tangible way to assess how frequently you practice self-care activities. It creates the opportunity to maintain positive mental health habits and well-being.

This self-care checkup allows you to document the frequency you practice self-care, categorizing these activities into five groups:
- *Emotional*
- *Physical*
- *Social*
- *Professional*
- *Spiritual*

Maintaining your self-care checkup worksheet will give you insight into the self-care deficits you may be indulging.

Worksheet #3

Self-Care Checkup (Cont.)

Instructions: Use the key on the following page to determine which level applies to your circumstances. Then, check the corresponding number as you make your way through the checklist.

Note: The following checklists are not exhaustive. If you think of ideas you'd like to add to the list, use the spaces provided.

Self-Care Checkup: Key

1	I rarely do this	I don't do this well
2	I sometimes do this	I'm average at doing this
3	I do this often	I do this very well
☐	I'd like to do this more often	I'd like to become better at this

Self-Care Checkup

	Emotional Self-Care	
1 2 3 ☐	Enjoying hobbies	
1 2 3 ☐	Taking a break from technology (e.g., email, social media, apps)	
1 2 3 ☐	Engaging in mentally stimulating conversations	
1 2 3 ☐	Learning and exploring new things (e.g., hobbies, foreign languages)	
1 2 3 ☐	Appreciating own talents, accomplishments, and strengths	
1 2 3 ☐	General emotional self-care	
1 2 3 ☐		

Self-Care Checkup

	Physical Self-Care	
1 2 3 ☐	Attending checkups/doctor's appointments (e.g., dental or GP checkups)	
1 2 3 ☐	Optimal sleep hygiene (i.e., sufficient sleep habits)	
1 2 3 ☐	Advocating for self when needs or concerns are ignored by medical professional(s)	
1 2 3 ☐	Drinking suitable amounts of water	
1 2 3 ☐	Resting when unwell	
1 2 3 ☐	General physical self-care	
1 2 3 ☐		

Self-Care Checkup

	Social Self-Care	
1 2 3 ☐	Making time for friends or family	
1 2 3 ☐	Staying in contact with distant connections (e.g., Skype, Facetime)	
1 2 3 ☐	Limiting time in uncomfortable environments to avoid social burn out	
1 2 3 ☐	Being intimate/romantic with partner	
1 2 3 ☐	Doing fun activities with others/ enjoyable group activities	
1 2 3 ☐	General social self-care	
1 2 3 ☐		

Self-Care Checkup

	Professional Self-Care	
1 2 3 ☐	Seeking support when it's required at work	
1 2 3 ☐	Maintaining a comfortable or pleasant work environment	
1 2 3 ☐	Balancing work and leisure activities	
1 2 3 ☐	Turning down unnecessary/ unreasonable tasks	
1 2 3 ☐	Pursuing further professional development opportunities	
1 2 3 ☐	General professional self-care	
1 2 3 ☐		

Self-Care Checkup

	Spiritual Self-Care	
1 2 3 ☐	Allocating quiet time for reflection	
1 2 3 ☐	Religious or spiritual practice	
1 2 3 ☐	Practicing gratitude and meditating	
1 2 3 ☐	Volunteering for charity/community	
1 2 3 ☐	Applying personal strengths, talents, or values	
1 2 3 ☐	General spiritual self-care	
1 2 3 ☐		

Bonus, Part A

Vision boards are a collage of different pictures and/or phrases used for visualizations. They are often used as a source of inspiration and motivation.

Instructions: *Create a vision board of what you want your life to look like in the next five years.*

Bonus, Part B

I really hope you enjoyed the journal prompts. I hope your journey to self-discovery was enjoyable. Just because you got to the end of this workbook doesn't mean your journey has ended here. Continue to learn about yourself every day. Look into other methods of exploration into yourself.

I highly suggest looking into guided meditation. It is a powerful tool and uncovers things your conscious mind has yet to reveal to you. One tip is to make sure you journal immediately after your meditation session. Write down the experience, colors, sounds, and images you saw. I have included a few extra pages, so you can write freely about your experience. It will be really fun!

Express Yourself...

Feel free to use the spaces provided on the next few pages to continue to jot down your thoughts.

Acknowledgements

I would like to send a special thanks and gratitude to my big sister, Cassidy Lee. Without her, this project would not have happened. Thank you for making my vision finally come to life.

Secondly, I would like to thank my mom, Robin Lee, also known as Ms. Cookie to me, for always supporting me through the good and bad. She always lets me know, "You got this!" She is the best mom ever!

I can't forget my Momo and Auntie Candy for making me feel like I can do anything I put my mind to. (I really have the best support system).

Lastly, thanks to my clients for inspiring this workbook. As I tell y'all in every session, you're awesome, and you got this!

About the Author

Danielle Lee is a licensed professional counselor supervisor and the owner of Solutions Focused Consulting. She has worked in MHRs since receiving her Master's in 2013 from Southeastern Louisiana University. She received her LPC in August 2015 and become an LPC-S in August 2018. Ms. Lee is currently working on her Ph.D. in Counselor Education and Supervision at Walden University.

In previous positions, she has served as a Wraparound Facilitator and Mental Health Professional (MHP), providing individual and family counseling service to clients in their homes, in schools, and surrounding communities. As a Clinical Manager, she provided clinical supervision and training to non-licensed staff. As a Utilization Manager, she reviewed outpatient behavioral health requests from providers credentialed with Managed Care Organizations. Ms. Lee has experience opening satellite offices of already established MHRs.

In addition, she has developed training manuals and facilitated several mandated trainings. She has been through several credentialing processes such as CARF and Louisiana MCOs, along with surveys conducted by MCOs to ensure the agencies were up to standards.

About the Company

Solutions Focused Consulting is a multifaceted agency, which offers a variety of mental health services. It offers telehealth sessions for clients in the states of Louisiana and Texas. More importantly, Solutions Focused Consulting aims to ensure its clients' mental health needs are being met.

Solutions Focused Consulting currently offers services for agencies that are in need of additional Licensed Mental Health Professional (LMHP) support as well.
The following is provided:
- Behavioral Health Assessments
- CA/LOCUS
- Outpatient Treatment Request/Authorizations for CPST and/or PSR
- Clinical Supervision
- Reviewing and Approving Client Notes
- Treatment Plans
- Discharge Paperwork

Stay Connected.

Thank you so much for going on this journey with me.

There is so much more I want to share. Be on the lookout for my next release in 2023.

To learn more about me or my practice, visit my website, or email me at solutionfocusedconsultingbr@gmail.com.

LET'S KEEP IN TOUCH.

WWW.SOLUTIONFOCUSEDCONSULTING.ORG